SAVED, SANCTIFIED, & SAME-GENDER LOVING

A Story-Journal to Spiritual Reconciliation

Derrick Tennial

LET'S RETHINK THAT
Atlanta, GA
www.letsrethinkthat.com

Derrick Tennial
dtennial@letrethinkthat.com
www.letsrethinkthat.com
Facebook: Derrick Tennial
Twitter & IG: dmtennial

Saved, Sanctified, & Same-Gender Loving:
A Story-Journal to Spiritual Reconciliation
Copyright © 2015

DEDICATION

"Then the word of the Lord came to me, saying: Before I formed you in the womb I knew you; before you were you born I sanctified you; I ordained you a prophet to the nations."

Jeremiah 1:5

This work is dedicated to all same-gender loving African-American males, especially those called into ministry, who have struggled to integrate their sexuality and spirituality into one reality.

"And when thou art converted, strengthen thy brethren."

Luke 22:31-32

TABLE OF CONTENTS

INSTRUCTIONS FOR READING

This story-journal is designed for the individual to have a personal encounter with himself. I strongly recommend that you read each story, highlight passages that speak to you. Following each story are Questions of Reconciliation designed to prompt you, the reader, to confront his spiritual and sexual identities. You may to spend some time (minutes, hours, days, even weeks) reflecting on each question before writing a response on the pages provided. The Questions of Reconciliation require you to do some soul searching, which may unearth deep-seeded issues from your past. Whatever the emotional response, release it as it part of the healing process. Please do not move onto the next story until you have answered all Questions of Reconciliation for that story. Remember, this process is not a sprint – it is a marathon, so take your time.

Let the process of reconciling your spiritual and sexual identities begin.

Dr. Travis Lee

"G.P.S. demands that you go in a certain direction; however, the Compass only tells you where you are. Everything else is up to you."

In traditional African spirituality, there is no divide between "sacred" and "secular." All elements of one's existential reality whether birth, life, love, relationships, sexuality, and even death are encompassed by traditional African spirituality as individual pieces of reality that together make up the whole. How can one accept the fact that he is a spiritual being, has a human existence, and can effectively navigate the sacred/secular divide that hyper post- modernity has created and subsequently placed in our collective consciousness, and not experience inner conflict? After all, in the annals of world history the concept of sacred versus secular is a relatively new one. Can one demonstrate Christian spirituality on Sunday and then leave it behind on Monday? Can one trust in the finished work of Christ on Calvary but not experience its effects with matters outside of the church, temple, or truth center? Can a Christian say that Christ has redeemed my soul but that redemption has nothing to do with my sexuality in general and my sexual orientation in particular? If Calvary is a complete work and if Christ has redeemed the total being, then would that redemption not work its way into the domain of a person's sexuality as well? If it does, then will that Same Gender Loving (SGL) person become straight? As SGL men who are children of the African Diaspora, it can be both problematic and traumatic to navigate the divide that exists between their Christian spirituality and their own sexuality. In this simple, yet substantive work, Derrick Tennial intermingles elements from his own life experiences with diagnostic questions designed to foster Contemplative Practice in order to bring a level of self-awareness that assists the reader in finding his position in that divide.

One should not mistakenly accept this author's magnum opus as a map to tell him where to go and what do to, but rather as a compass to help one to pin point his exact location in this dangerous divide between sexuality and spirituality so that he can plot his/her own course to the safety of reconciliation. When one can live in the wonderful assurance that is rooted in spirituality that is reconciled with his sexuality,

10

then there is harmony. When one can live in an increasingly secular society but effectively demonstrate Christian spirituality, thereby maintaining balance between the sacred and the secular, then he is blessed. The goal of this book is not to get the reader to agree with every perspective or viewpoint presented by the author, but to stimulate thought, self-examination, contemplation, dialogue, and critical reflection in an effort to help others navigate "the great divide" that seemingly exits between the two worlds of sexuality (secular) and spirituality (sacred). So let this compass guide you to self-awareness, reconciliation, and ultimately to safety.

INTRODUCTION

At the age of six, I became consciously and acutely aware of my attraction to the same-sex. One evening, my aunt's boyfriend came over to visit, and I recall swinging between my aunt's boyfriend's legs and liking it and him more than I should have. Noting my behavior as queer for a little boy and out of concern, my aunt informed my mother, my uncles, and the family matriarch – my grandmother. Standing in my grandmother's kitchen, I was made painfully aware that homosexuality would not be tolerated in this family and that it was sinful in the eyesight of God; in fact, it was more than sinful – it was an abomination! My six-year old mind did not know the meaning of that word, but the way my grandmother said it made it sound worse than death. I cried, internalizing feelings of shame, embarrassment, guilt, and condemnation because deep down in my six-year old heart I knew I was pre- destined to be a same-gender loving African-American male...

How many African-American boys tell their family and friends, "When I grow up, I want to be gay?" For an African-American male to make such a statement is the same as proclaiming, "I want to be a pariah, a leper, a social outcast." However, this is exactly the way many African-American males are made to feel if they show what is considered to be the slightest homosexual or effeminate tendency (i.e. a dislike for playing outside or spending too much time with female counterparts instead of with the other males). These internalized feelings of shame, embarrassment, guilt, and condemnation cement feelings of inadequacy in their very souls, which causes them to search for ways to earn and retain the love and acceptance of their family, the community, and ultimately God. They attempt to conform to established societal norms and family's expectations. Tortured by the fact that they have these innate desires, they fail miserably attempting to suppress them all while endeavoring to be pleasing in God's eyesight and to live up to everyone's expectations, which brings their spirituality and sexuality into continuous conflict and causes them to navigate between two worlds: saved and sanctified in one and same-gender loving in the other. I navigate between these two worlds.

I was born in the "Bible Belt" and raised in fear and admonition of the Lord! On a Friday night during a summer revival at the age of twelve, I accepted Jesus Christ as my Lord and Savior. For the two days leading up to my Sunday morning baptism, I felt strangely warm; in the words of gospel artist Darryl Coley, I sensed God was "preparing me for something I couldn't handle..." At the age of nineteen, I accepted the call into Christian ministry. By this time, I had united with a Pentecostal church and subsequently received the baptism of the Holy Ghost with "the signs of speaking in other tongues as the spirit of God gave utterance." Over the next several years, I served in various capacities in the church: new members' intake, children's church instructor, youth pastor, in the male Introduction 7 chorus, in the men's ministry, on the praise team, pastor's personal adjutant, district secretary of one the denomination's districts, and adult Sunday school instructor. I did everything from serving at the back door as an as a greeter to ushering to preaching in the pulpit. At the age of twenty-five, I was ordained an elder in the church. Psalms 37:37 says, "Mark the perfect man," and to many, I was the example of a perfect man – young, educated, and striving to live Holy for the Lord. My future was beyond bright! I was loved and respected by the church community, my family, among my professional colleagues, and I was beginning to build a reputation as a leader in the community-at-large. I even had several beautiful women after me – two who claimed, "The Lord said you are my husband!" Yeah, right!?!? However, near the advent of this potentially promising future, I walked away because of the continuous conflict between my spirituality and sexuality. I was saved, sanctified, and same-gender loving.

Through my stories, I hope to give voice to many saved, sanctified, and same-gendered loving men (and women) who are in constant conflict with their spirituality and sexuality - navigating between the two worlds. My stories are nothing more than illustrations of how I have struggled to live in these contradictory spaces, and in recent years, how I have sought to reconcile these two factions. I hope that these stories and the Questions of Reconciliation at the end of each story will provoke the same- gender loving male to examine his past, present, and future, whether he classifies himself as gay, bi, down-lo, transgender, transsexual, straight or as someone likes to "mess around with dudes on the side." I also hope that these stories will evoke conversations among African-American same-gender loving brothers in order to effect change within and outside of our social networks, to promote a paradigm shift that will cause both entities   to recognize African-American same-gender loving males as a   marginalized group historically oppressed by their own- African-American community and church, and to bring about healing, love, and acceptance of all African-American men, regardless of sexual orientation.

WHY I QUIT WRITING

I quit writing. During my sophomore year of college, while sitting in front of my laptop in my dorm room, I made a conscious decision to stop writing. I had been an avid writer before I even knew how to write. I had had a love affair with words before I even knew how to speak. That day, in my dorm room, I ended my writing career before it had ever begun. I quit writing! Why did I quit? The answer is simply; it is the same now as it was then. I quit writing because I couldn't deal with me.

I was twenty years old then and had dreams of becoming a professional writer and a published author. Growing up, I was a fan of the daytime soaps Young and the Restless, Bold and the Beautiful, As the World Turns, and Guiding Light, as well as nighttime soaps Dynasty, Knots Landing, The Colbys, and others, I dreamt of a career writing; I would pen stories for my favorite soap characters. The soaps were a source of inspiration; I loved the drama and suspense of them so much so that as a teenager I created my own serials and wrote stories filled with melodrama. I became as engulfed in my stories as

I did in my daytime and nighttime soaps. I remember purposely getting sick at school so I could go home and watch Trey and Sloane's Charles and Diana- sequel wedding on *Capitol*. (That was long before the days of DVR's; VCR's were relatively new and too expensive for my parents to afford). As I made the transition from elementary to junior high school, my writing became especially important to me. I wrote to sort out my feelings as my world began changing`. I was in junior high school now, I had a new little brother, and I had discovered...boys! My writing allowed me to create a world all my own; I would retreat to other parts of the house if someone entered the room where I was writing. My mother sensed that I was using my writing as a means of escape, and she called me out on it. She thought that I had retreated into this world simply because I was having difficulty dealing with the reality that I now had to share my parents' love and attention with a new sibling after having been an only child for almost 13 years, but it was more than that. However, I felt like she'd violated my space and my place with that confrontation, so I became somewhat ashamed and embarrassed by my thoughts and my feelings. Nevertheless, throughout junior and senior high school, I continued writing. I even wrote and produced my first play in the ninth grade and my first documentary in eleventh grade which became the inspiration for my doctoral dissertation. By the time I graduated high school, I recognized that my stories were missing something. My melodramas were born and developed purely out of my imagination and not from any kind of life experience – I had just begun to live. I wanted my stories to be real, birthed out of my life's experience, and have substance

I sat at my desk that sweltering June day just staring at my computer determined to create a new serial in which all of the characters would embody parts of my personality. My life had been pretty ordinary, with the exception of the last two years, which had been turbulent to say the least. The December after I graduated high school, I had my first sexual and homosexual encounter. Long before pop singer Katie Perry sang "I Kissed a Girl," I kissed a boy. It was a kiss that changed my life and popped the lid off of lifelong homosexual suppression. I experienced my first two same-sex relationships, both with directors of college choirs, (Yeah, I know...it's always those damn choir directors!) within months of each other. The first guy broke my heart, I broke the heart of the second guy because I was gay and I didn't know how to deal with being gay and being in a relationship with him. To make matters worse, the revelation of my homosexuality made my mama's blood pressure shoot through the roof... literally. Lord, I don't want to kill my mama! Furthermore, growing up I had been taught that homosexuality was wrong, it was sinful, it was an abomination and all homosexuals were going to hell. Surely, I didn't want to go to hell? Dealing with all of these warnings or morbid thoughts caused me to have incessant headaches because I was conflicted. I didn't know what to do or which way to turn. In the words of Cher, "If I could turn back time, if I could find a way," I would have never kissed a boy. I just wanted it all to go away! And made it go away, I did...or so I thought!

I sat at my desk pondering, pontificating, where I was and where I wanted to go. I remembered the scripture I prayed when the first choir director abruptly ended our relationship (1) because he was on the rebound from a previous relationship and (2) because he wanted to live for the Lord leaving me in a broken state of confusion.

Sitting at my desk, I began with that scripture and I prayed desperately to find my way out of that dark abyss: "If my people, who are called by name, shall humble themselves, and pray, seek my face, and turn from their wicked ways, then I will hear from heaven, and will forgive their sin and heal their land" (2 Chronicles 7:14). And sure enough, God delivered me out of that place!

I sat there thinking about a few months after my deliverance from the situation with my first boyfriend, I left my second boyfriend for the same reason my first boyfriend left me: I wanted to live for the Lord; I wanted to walk upright before him, and I couldn't do that being gay! I wanted to maintain the love and respect of my family, friends, and community, and especially the wonderful new church I had joined that taught holiness and sanctification. What would happen if family and friends found out (as if they did not already know) that I had had same-sex experiences? My squeaky-clean image would be dirtied. What would happen to my aspirations of becoming a community leader? No one would take serious a "fudge-packer" (a term used by one of my former female church members who was oblivious to my sexuality). What would happen if the church found out that its new minister was a sodomite?

I sat there at my desk looking at a blank Microsoft Works page, and I made a conscious decision to quit writing because I could not deal with the real – because I could not deal with me. I closed my laptop and simultaneously closed that chapter of my sexuality. I decided that it was indeed, and would stay a part of my past. No more would I think about it. No more would I even associate with people involved in it. I even renounced that I was ever homosexual to my mother. And I certainly would not ever write about it again, for writing about it would validate that those experiences took place and would serve as concrete evidence that my past experiences could destroy my future. From that moment forward, my same-sex dalliances were finished once and for all! I would be the man that God called me to be. Little did I know at that time the man God call me to be is a homosexual man. Eight years later, I started writing again because I was learning to deal with the real – I was learning to deal with me.

QUESTIONS OF RECONCILIATION

I am a firm believer that "covered things don't heal well." For years, my inability to confront my sexuality delayed my healing and being made whole in many aspects of my life. It even robbed me of some of my goals and dreams. Consider these questions:

What part(s) of your personality (inclusive or exclusive of your sexuality) have you yet to confront? Why?

What has your inability to confront your sexuality cost you?

PAPER DOLLS

Recently, one of my students made a profound statement during an impromptu discussion on homosexuality and how toys are used in the socialization of children. She argued that allowing boys to play with dolls teaches them how to be gentle with women. Her comment literally blew me away! To many in society allowing boys to play with dolls is socially taboo. It is unthinkable, unconceivable, and viewed as totally and undeniably wrong! To allow a boy to play with a doll is to destine him to be a gay! However, out of the mouth of this seventeen-year-old babe came a prospective I had never considered, especially since I liked playing with dolls as a young boy. I can remember as early as four years old, going to the home of my great-aunt, who had three young daughters and being allowed to play with my cousin's baby doll. I loved to comb the baby's blond corn silk hair, styling it in any fashion I wanted. I loved dressing the baby doll equally as well. I think because I was so young, my great-aunt, her husband, or her daughters did not think much about the fact that I was a boy playing with a doll. However, my affinity for dolls continued as I got older. I remember that several of my female childhood friends had extensive Barbie doll collections – every Barbie you could imagine from Malibu Barbie to Wedding Fantasy Barbie and all in between. I liked going over to their houses because it was the only time I got to play with dolls... somewhat "openly." I knew that our play would not be interrupted until it was time for me leave because our parents were engaged in "grown-folks talk." I hated for our playtime to end because it signaled the temporary end to my love affair with Barbie. I had no dolls of my own because by that age I was in school and had been socialized to believe that boys had to play with trucks, cars, action figures, guns, and such. Let there be no mistake - I had a love for these toys and played with these items created to develop my manhood, but I still liked doll.

My mother had a doll collection of her own that she kept in a box in her closet. From time to time, I would dig out her Barbie dolls from the bottom of the box and play with them, not only styling their hair, but cutting their hair as well. I am certain that at some point my mother discovered that P.J. (one of Barbie's female counterparts), who started out with long, flowing sandy blond hair cascading down her back, mysteriously ended up with a greasy shoulder-length bob. After each of my play sessions, I would carefully return P.J. to her packaging and placed her at the bottom of my mother's toy box. My affair with P.J. and other dolls lasted until the latter end of my pre-teen years when I finally "grew out of it." However, in the years prior, not only did I find my way into my mother's doll box, but I also found my way into the aunt's toy chest. My aunt, my mother's youngest sister, is only ten years older than I, and also had Barbie dolls she'd kept from her childhood. While over at my grandmother's house, I would sneak into my aunt's toy chest and play with her dolls, hiding this from my grandmother and my uncles. I already knew how they felt about "sissies" and I knew that if my doll play was discovered, I would be labeled and ridiculed and criticized. Therefore, I always took steps to conceal the fact that I liked to play with dolls.

One day while in my aunt's toy chest looking for Barbie, I discovered Barbie's replacement – paper dolls. There were five cardboard figures – a mother, a father, a daughter, a son, and a dog. Along with these five cardboard figures were paper outfits with these little tabs on them that I could connect to the paper dolls to dress them. The discovery of my aunt's paper dolls opened up a whole new world of imagination for me. Not only could I dress the dolls in various outfits, but now I could design their own clothing. I got a blue two-pocket folder and housed my paper dolls and all their clothing in it. From that moment forward, wherever I went, my blue folder was sure to follow...along with paper and crayons, so that I could design fabulous new outfits for my paper doll family. Better yet, I could play with them somewhat in the open unlike I could never play with Barbie. I was an only child and played well alone. My family would think that I was just coloring, (which I loved to do) when in fact I was designing clothes for my paper dolls. There was a tradeoff where the paper dolls were concerned: the paper dolls did not have any hair I could comb, but designing clothes for them more than made up the hair styling loss. I so enjoyed designing clothes for my papers dolls. It was through playing with my paper dolls that I knowingly chose my first career aspiration – fashion design. I dreamed of designing awesome couture for people, much like the clothing which Krystle and Alexis wore on Dynasty. In addition to that, my doll play also sparked my interesting in writing short stories. I would use my paper dolls to create elaborate stories that contained all of the essential elements of plot development – basic situation, complication, rising actions, climax, falling action, and resolution. Even though it was oral, I was an awesome storyteller, and my paper dolls helped me to dream and fantasize about what I could be in life. Even though I was beginning to understand the expectations and limitations of family and society, I still believed that I could do anything I wanted to do and go anywhere I wanted to go. I knew that my childhood secret play could one day become celebrated work. So I took pride in my secretive doll play, until all I held sacred was threatened once when I spent the weekend at my grandmother's house....

Overnight bags were not common. If you were going to spend a night or two away from home, you simply threw your belongings in an old shopping bag, and you were on your way. This is exactly what I did when I went over my grandmother's house. Not only did I throw my clothes in an old shopping bag, but I placed my special blue folder containing my beloved paper dolls in that bag as well. Once at my grandmother's house, I got my clothes out of that shopping bag, but I left my blue folder with my paper dolls in the bag as an extra precaution to conceal my secret play activity. Wherever I went in the house, I took the shopping bag with me. No one questioned what was in the bag. Everyone assumed that my toys were in it, until my grandmother accidentally threw away that old shopping bag the next morning...

I had set my shopping bag at the top of the steps while I went into the bathroom to bathe. Not thirty minutes later when I came out of the bathroom, my shopping bag had vanished. It was gone! I retraced my steps thinking that I had left it in my aunt's room where I had slept the night before, but it wasn't there! I tried to remain calm. I looked in my uncles' room, thinking I might have accidentally put it in there, but it wasn't there. I began to panic. I even checked my grandmother's bedroom. It wasn't there. I panicked! I became frantic! As I came out of my grandmother's room, she had just made it to the upstairs' landing. Seeing my panic-ridden face, she immediately asked me in her strong, heavy voice that would strike fear in the heart of God, "What's the matter?" In that split second, I realized a fear greater than my missing paper dolls and the loss of them; it was actually the fear of my being exposed.

After catching my breath, I answered her – my voice quivering, "My bag! My bag is gone!"

"What bag?" she yelled.

"My bag...that was right here at the top of the stairs!" I stuttered.

"What was in the bag?" Why did she have to ask that question? The only thing I could reply was, "My toys," as I began to cry.

"I must have thrown it away with the rest of the trash that was sitting up here."

My heart dropped, and I began to cry even more as I realized that my paper dolls were in the sea of garbage in the dumpster in the parking lot behind the building. As I stood there crying hysterically, my grandmother sprang into action to recover "my toys." I followed her downstairs to the backdoor. She looked outside and saw, "Lil' Larry." Lil' Larry lived down the hill in another unit and happened to be passing by. He was a teenager (late teens), but no one would have known that unless you really knew him; he was short and small enough to climb into the dumpster and retrieve my bag which is exactly what he did. To say the least, I was relieved to have my shopping bag back in my possession. Even more so, my secret was still safe, but not for long...

Several weeks later, while cleaning my room, as she routinely did without permission, my mother discovered my paper dolls. There was no such thing as privacy in our house; my mother made sure that I knew so. If I wanted to keep anything a secret, I had to hide it, but somehow she always managed to find everything. While I was a teenager, she told me, "There's nothing that you do that I don't know about." Boy was she right! I was in another room when the discovery was made and from the way she called my name – "Derrick Marcel Tennial" - I could tell I was in trouble.

"Ma'am," I answered as I eased into my room, afraid for my life. In her hands were two things: my daddy's leather belt and one of my latest paper doll fashion designs – a purple and orange swing dress. The gig was up! I don't remember exactly what she said to me; all I remember was my daddy's leather belt, her indignant tone, and the certainty that I was going to get an "ass-whooping" if I did not obey. I do remember my dress being cut in two by my daddy's belt and watching it feather to the floor in two parts. After that day, I never played with my paper dolls again...

According to society's norms and expectations, boys shouldn't play with girls' toys. The fear is that little boys playing with girls' toys foster effeminate qualities in boys. Child's play, in general, regardless of the gender-specific toys involved, may unearth talents that could develop into profitable careers in that child-turned adult's life. Who knows what I might have done, if I had not been made to feel ashamed or been socialized to believe that as a male child, I was doing something wrong? I could have been the next Willi Smith, Calvin Klein, or Gianni Versace. The irony is that society scolds and ridicules boys for playing with girls' toys, but totally accepts girls playing with boys' toys. Little girls who play with masculine toys are branded future feminists who will change traditional gender roles in our society and they are also heralded as heroines for doing just that. Yet little boys who play with feminine toys are branded as future faggots, charged with advancing the moral decay of our society. It seems as if no one is afraid that girls will develop masculine qualities and become lesbians. How many times have we heard the rationale, "Oh, she's just a tomboy," but no one wants to hear the expression, "Oh, he's just a tom girl!" Since I was already displaying non-traditional tendencies, my mother may have feared that my doll-play cemented my future as a homosexual. I cannot and will not blame my mother for acting as she thought best, for she was simply conforming to the societal norms and expectations she had been taught. I fully recognize that perhaps what my mother was trying to do, when she threatened me with the belt and used it as a double-edged sword to cut my paper-doll design in two, was to protect me from future hurt by what she perceived as a lifestyle choice. Or perhaps she was afraid that my homosexual tendencies would bring shame and ridicule upon her and the rest of my family. I am not sure; however, I am sure of this: No child comes with an instruction manual, especially if the child is going to grow up and be homosexual. How does a mother explain to her seven- year- old African-American son, who already has one strike against him because of his skin color and who is now exhibiting homosexual tendencies, that he is destined to be "despised and rejected by men; a man of sorrows, and acquainted with grief" all because he is different– all because he likes to play with paper dolls?

In our society, we laud the truth...except when that truth does not conform to the expectations of others or the society in which we live. Oftentimes, we would rather believe a lie than accept the truth about whom and what we are. Consider these questions:

How old were you when you discovered you were attracted to the same-sex?

How old were you when someone in your family discovered your same-sex attraction?

Do you think the discovery of your homosexual tendencies altered your relationship with your family?

Did you have any aspiration(s) that you were discouraged from pursuing because they did not fit into traditional masculine roles?

"I'm moving you out of the shadow of your pastor!" God clearly and plainly spoke to me during worship service the morning after I was suspended from the ministerial alliance for the mismanagement of a church project. Many of the other ministers were shocked by the announcement by the assistant pastor in an impromptu meeting, but I was relieved. For four years straight, I had dedicated myself totally to the church. I was there every time the doors opened. I served at all three Sunday worship services and taught adult Sunday school in between. I was there on Wednesday nights for Bible study or in my capacity as youth pastor, I taught Bible study to the youth. I was there on Friday nights to lead or participate in corporate prayer. I was there on any given day of the week for meetings or special events. All of this, in addition to serving as my pastor's personal adjutant, attending undergraduate, then graduate school full-time AND working full-time as well. I was as dedicated as they come. Please do not misunderstand: I love to serve. I am a servant with a servant's heart, but I now recognize that I was totally burned out. So when the Lord told me, "I am moving you out of the shadow of your pastor," I merely thought that this would be an opportunity to rest, but that is not what God meant at all.

I was suspended for a month. According to the terms of my suspension, I still had to attend worship services, but I could not serve in any capacity: I could not teach Sunday school, I could not lead any worship service, and I could not serve as my pastor's personal adjutant. I could not even sit with the other ministers. When the suspension was lifted, I was refreshed and rejuvenated and expected to pick right up where I left off; it didn't happen, for a shift had occurred...

In my absence, church life continued to flow. Now, the people who had covered for me during my suspension were reluctant to relinquish "my positions." I, the one whose gifts had made room for him, felt totally and completely out of place - like a fish out of water. "No one is indispensable!" I heard the voice of my high school music teacher who repeatedly said this when the choir refused to cooperate at rehearsals. She was right! Once a member of the pastor's inner circle, I was suddenly on the outside looking in. I cried out, "God, what does this mean?" I didn't know what to do! There had been a time when I knew exactly what I was doing before, during, and after any given service. Not anymore! I didn't realize that so much of my identity was wrapped up in the church. Now, I didn't know who I was or where I was going anymore.

Even though I had worked so hard to present this "holier than thou" facade, that was not who I was. I was an imposter – a same gender loving man, using the church and my titles of minister and elder to mask my true sexual identity! I imitated my pastor in all aspects of my church life because in my eyes he was the premier example of a saved, sanctified, spirit-filled heterosexual man - an image I desperately tried to replicate because I could not deal with my own image.

"I'm moving you out of the shadow of your pastor!" Now I began to understand that all that was happening around me was a part of God's plan. He had to get me away from the shadow – and out of an earshot of my pastor's voice – so I could clearly hear His voice. God knew that I had great love, respect, and adoration for my pastor, and that I would have done just about anything he told me without question or thought. I gave my pastor too much decision-making power over my life instead of following the voice of God. I had listened to my pastor when it came to moving to an apartment close to the church. I had done the same when it came to deciding whether to attend seminary in my hometown or to move to Atlanta several years earlier before I actually moved. I chose to attend seminary and graduate school in my hometown, so I could continue to serve my pastor and the church. But now a shift had occurred...

There was no going back to the way things were before the suspension. God moved and moved swiftly. In a casual conversation with a friend who unpredictably became my boyfriend (that's the subject of another story), the idea of moving to Atlanta unexpectedly resurfaced. We both shared our individual hopes and dreams for wanting to move. Before the end of our conversation, we created a timeline for the move. I left his apartment that day a bit skeptical. I couldn't believe that I was really considering uprooting myself and starting over. Even though things at the church were not at best, I had invested too much! In spite of the difficulties at the moment, in the back of my mind, I still believed that my path had been laid before me at this church. I thought I was destined to work my way up through the ranks of the church and eventually pastor the church. After all, I was the one who was most like my pastor. Internally, I questioned, God, is this you or this me, attempting to run away from this graven image I have created? I had visited Atlanta enough to know that it was a haven for the African-American gay community. Am I thinking about moving to Atlanta, so I can live openly gay? Is this move in your perfect will?

Sometimes it seemingly takes God a very long time to answer; other times he answers quickly. The answers to my questions came when a fellow ministerial colleague and mentor with whom I had shared nothing concerning a possible move to Atlanta prophesied that "the move" was of God. Now I fully and completely understood what God meant when he said, "I am moving you out of the shadows of your pastor." He allowed the suspension so I could hear His voice, so I would be open when He gave me directions to leave the city, so I could continue the work of reconciliation of my sexuality and spirituality within me. Immediately, I told my family and select members of the church that I would be moving to Atlanta. In the final months of my tenure, I served less and less in various roles in the ministry. I was all but a lay member again, no longer sitting with the elders and ministers. My last Sunday there also marked my seven-year anniversary of the day I joined the church.

"I'm moving you out of the shadow of your pastor!" My friend- turned-boyfriend and I moved to Atlanta together and roomed together, more for financial reasons than for romantic ones. I moved, searching for someone I had never really known...me!

QUESTIONS OF RECONCILIATION

God has known who and what we are since before we were born into this world. However, instead of accepting the truth that is right before us, we sometimes choose an alternate path because we desire others' adoration and respect more than we desire the adoration and respect of God. Consider these questions:

Is the identity you have your own or one that you have adopted?

Are you on the path to the destiny you have chosen or the destiny God has chosen for you?

Managing the Thorn:
The Damascus Road Experience

"God, You promised You would take this away from me!"

"No, I didn't! You only assumed that I would!"

I was driving back to my hometown after having a tryst with a young man who attended a college an hour and a half away. I had met him on the local chat line a week or so earlier. Yes, I could have found someone local to "kick it with," but I was always taught that you don't eat and Sugar-Honey-Ice-Tea in the same place. I could not run the risk of someone finding out about my sexual encounters, so I met guys outside of my immediate area. Driving back that night, I was despondent and disappointed because I had… slipped. I had somehow managed to keep my homoerotic desires in check for four years, yet now it seemed that I was losing my grip. I had started a year earlier with a mere slip with a friend and before I knew it, I found myself frequenting the chat line and having secret encounters with men in-state and out of state.

After this latest encounter, I was determined that I had to bring my flesh back under restraint; I was spiraling out of control, doing things unbecoming of a minister – a man of GOD! Not only was I disappointed in myself, but I was also disappointed in God. He had not lived up to His promise – to deliver me from homosexuality. Three years after I had walked away from it, it was seemingly back with a vengeance! So while driving home from my rendezvous, I decided to confront God about being slack concerning His promises.

"God," I indignantly called, "You promised me that You would take this away from me!"

God simply and calmly replied, "No, I didn't! You only assumed that I would!"

I was suddenly crushed and confused to say the least! Since my pre-teen years, I had been praying that God would take away my homosexual desires because I was ashamed of who and what I was one. I felt so ashamed that when I prayed, asking God for deliverance in my dark bedroom in the middle of the night, I couldn't even say the words "homosexual," "homosexuality," "gay," or anything related to the subject. I would pray, "God, please take away

48

these sinful desires. I know that it is wrong for me to be this way!"

Now, after all these years, God tells me that I only assumed that He would deliver me from my lustful, immoral desires? Did this mean that He was not going to do what I had been earnestly praying for and asking him to do for years? Did this mean that the God, the same one who had delivered Moses and the children of Israel, was not going to deliver me? If that was the case, then why did I pray in the first place? What in the hell was I to do now?

God was silent for the remainder of my trip back home. After that night, I tried my best to figure out just exactly what God was trying to say to me. What was clear was that I had made an erroneous assumption. I had assumed that God would deliver me from something, that perhaps He had absolutely no intention of doing. I questioned: What does God's lassitude mean for me personally? Does it mean that will struggle with homosexuality for the rest of my life? Does it mean that my ministry will change or possibly end? Many people in the church, particularly the Pentecostal church, still believe that homosexuality is a demonic spirit that needs to be cast out of a believer. God's statement to me that night on the interstate created more questions than answers in my mind. I didn't know what to think; I didn't know what to pray. All I could do was to cry out in anguish, "God, help me!" I had a Damascus Road-like experience, similar to Saul's, who embraced his Roman (gentile) name and identity of Paul on that Damascus Road, thus moving from a Christ persecutor to a Christ proclaimer. The question I was left with was: Who am I? What am I?

While I waited on God to speak and provide new revelation, I tried to subject control over my flesh, to little avail. I continued to rendezvous with various men while becoming more and more frustrated that God's wisdom and guidance had yet to make an appearance in my life or resolve my dilemma.

Several weeks after my Damascus Road-like experience, God spoke again through the voice of my pastor one Wednesday night at Bible study. My pastor had been conducting a series on spiritual gifts, and I fully expected him to continue teaching in that vein. However, when he took to the pulpit that night, he proclaimed that in his time of prayer, meditation, and preparation, God had taken him in another direction. He read two passages of scripture from the King James Bible: "For this thing I besought the Lord thrice, that it might depart from me. And he [the Lord] said unto me, my grace is sufficient for thee; for my strength is made perfect in weakness." My pastor then announced his topic of discussion for the evening, titled "Managing the Thorn." I nearly jumped out of my seat because immediately I knew that this was the word from the Lord on which I had been waiting since my Damascus Road-like experience. My pastor gave the historical context of the lesson which involved the Apostle Paul and how to manage the thorn – a message he had received from Satan to prevent him from exalting himself and not giving God the glory. The first thing my pastor told the congregation was that to learn how to manage the thorn, you must first acknowledge that there is a thorn. He stated, "Everyone has a thorn; it might be the same as others, but it may also be something totally different. It is the one element that keeps us from being perfect."

Immediately, I knew what my thorn was; it was my issue with my sexuality. I had always felt that I would be the "perfect" man if it were not for my need to be with other men. My conflict with my sexuality hindered me from being the absolute best I could be. I took notes vigorously, as my pastor expounded upon how we must first acknowledge to ourselves that the thorn exists. He then explained that not only must we acknowledge the existence of the thorn to ourselves, but we must also acknowledge its existence to God!

I questioned: What sense does that make? God is all seeing, all knowing, and all-present! Why must I admit to him something he already knows?

It was as if my pastor heard the questions I was asking within myself. God spoke through him and provided an immediate answer. Even though God knows and sees everything, some things He just wants you to tell Him in order to create trust and intimacy between the two of you. He wants no secrets or barriers between you and Him. As my pastor's words ministered to me, I realized that even though I had had same-sex relationships and experiences, I had never really acknowledged my sexual identity to myself or to God. Even in making my requests to him for deliverance, I could not even use the words "homosexual," "homosexuality," "gay," or any other related term. Somehow...some way...I was still in total denial!

After Bible study that evening, the word continued to marinate in my spirit. I could not get over the fact that I needed to acknowledge my sexuality to myself and to God. I believed I could acknowledge it to myself, but acknowledge it to GOD? All my life, I had grown up to believe and had been taught that homosexuality was a sin, a filthy abomination in the sight of God, and now I needed to acknowledge my homosexuality, my sin, to HIM!?!? God forbid! I took my best friend, who belonged to the same church and had also gone to Bible study with me, to Kroger afterwards to do some grocery shopping. While she shopped, I continued to think about acknowledging the thorn in my life to myself...and to God. Could I do it? Should I do it? What would happen if I did it? I concluded that there was only one way to find out...

I stopped in my tracks right there in Kroger, looked up, and made honest and open confession at light-speed to God: "God, I like men! I like them my height or shorter, light skinned with pretty eyes. I like kissing a man, holding a man, and caressing his body...." Nonstop I continued addressing God, in the middle of Aisle Eight at Kroger. For about five minutes, I unapologetically confessed to my heavenly Father that I was a man -loving homosexual. No sooner had I finished my confession, in the realm of the spirit, I felt the veil in my temple rip in two, just as it had when Jesus died on the cross, giving to believer's free access and an intimate relationship with the Father, without the need of an intercessory priest or a required sacrifice! In addition, I felt that my potential relationship with God reach its fullest potential - that nothing would separate me from the love of God. Something truly remarkable happened in Kroger on Aisle Eight - eight being God's number of new beginnings. God began the process of reconciling my sexuality and my spirituality.

Slowly, I began to accept that I was a same-gender loving male! I still did not understand all of what my confession to God meant for me personally and for my ministry, but I did begin to understand that God was calling me to a higher consciousness. First and foremost, He had called me to be honest with myself and with Him, but like many people, I really did not receive the fullness of the message the first time. So like the children of Israel, I had to wonder around in the wilderness. I had had to have another Damascus Road-like experience...

Three Years Later

"You're a hypocrite!" God said to me one day out of the blue as I was driving down Collier Road in Atlanta on the way home.

"I'm a hypocrite?" I asked.

"You're a hypocrite!" he repeated!

"God, I have served you all I know how. I have been faithful and committed to you and your work. How am I a hypocrite?" I exclaimed!

"You have not been totally honest with Me about your sexuality and what has been going on in your life!" He then asked me a question. "Has you being gay ever stopped you from being what I say you would become or doing what I said you would do?"

I took a quick snapshot of my life, looking at what I have been able to achieve in spite of my sexuality issue and then I replied to Him, "No!"

"Then why are you still worried about it?"

In that moment, I realized that I had matured very little beyond my Damascus Road-like and Kroger-Aisle Eight experiences. God had been calling me to a greater consciousness so that I could reconcile my sexuality and my spirituality. Yet, I was still trying to hide from Him like Adam did when he heard God's voice in garden because he knew he was naked. Now God insisted that I move beyond the mere confession I had made in Kroger's; He demanded to be included in every aspect of my life. He wanted me to acknowledge Him in all my ways, so he could direct my path.

God was right! I was a hypocrite because of my dishonesty with Him, my worrying about the impact my sexuality could have on my ministry and future success, my failure to realize that my steps were being ordered by God and that I could not rely on my church work and good deeds; but rather stand on my faith in Him and my relationship with Him. I was a hypocrite in the truest sense of the word. Wounded and open, I listened as God asked me another question that if answered honestly, would not just heal me, but would begin to make me whole.

He asked, "Has you being gay ever stopped you from becoming what I said you would become or doing what I said you would do?" In an instance, I took a panoramic view of my life and saw that every goal I had ever set and every goal He had ever set for me, I had attained with a spirit of excellence – no less.

So then I solemnly replied to God's question, "No!"

God rhetorically asked, "Then why are you still worried about it?" It was in that moment I stopped worrying about whether my sexuality was pleasing in God's eyes, and I began to focus on acknowledging Him in all my ways so He could continue to direct my life. My sexuality is innate part of who I am – something I did not ask for or desire. It is a part of the uniform I was issued before I was formed in my mother's belly. It is my "thorn"– a perceived weakness in the eyes of others – that God uses to perfect his strength by bringing health and healing to a marginalized group of men and women whose potential has been minimized because we have been historically and subconsciously made to feel that we are not worth of relationship with God unless we subject ourselves to or succumb to societal norms.

QUESTIONS OF RECONCILIATION

Many of us have been taught to see God through other people's eyes without ever trying to understand who and what He is for ourselves. Consider these questions:

How do you see God?

How do you think God sees you?

Do you ask for His guidance and wisdom in all things, including when it comes to the partners with whom you become involved?

Do you think you can use your sexuality to glorify God?

The fairytale died! During a visit to my hometown of Memphis to attend the graduation of my twin cousins, I experienced a death like no other. It was an unexpected death. It was something that I never expected to die. I expected it to live "happily ever after." However, it didn't. While sitting at a computer at the city's main library, the unfathomable happened. The fairytale died.

From a very young age, girls and boys alike are socialized to believe that fairytales come true. From Snow White and the Seven Drafts to The Princess and the Frog to The Little Mermaid to Sleeping Beauty to Aladdin to my all-time favorite, and the mother of all fairytales Cinderella, we have been taught to laude and have faith in the central storyline: the damsel in distress, after being rescued from a dire situation by the handsome, debonair, and savoir-faire prince, falls in love with the prince, they marry, and live happily ever after. This fairytale is reinforced through television shows including sitcoms, dramedies, and my all-time personal favorite, soap operas. However, in real life as I have discovered, the fairytale is just that – a tale, a lie, a concocted story; children all over the world are taught to believe in something that is not rooted in reality.

What is even more fascinating for me isn't the fact that I am a male who once bought into this myth of romance, but I am a same-gender loving male, who like females, believed that a prince would ride into my life on his horse and literally swept me off my feet. I believed in the fairytale so much so, that time and time again I sought to create and recreate fairytale-like moments in my relationships– only to have my fairytale ending dissolve or disintegrate time and time again. Like Prince Charming, I am the total package – tall, relatively handsome, professional, spiritual and cultured. Repeatedly, I am asked the questions, "Why are you alone and why hasn't someone snatched you up? Nine times out of ten, my reply is simply, "I don't know." But after angrily pondering this question again and again, after tirelessly consulting with friends, enemies, frenemies, former loves, one-night stands, or potential boyfriends who jilted me, I have come to the conclusion that very few of them want the prince.

As desirable as he may be in the fairytale, very few can actually handle the prince. Why? There are certain duties, responsibilities, and expectations that come with wanting, loving and having him. The irony is these duties, responsibilities, and expectations are not required by the prince. He would simply accept the one he loves unconditionally; the duties, responsibilities, and expectations are an innate part of the prince that calls his potential prince to a higher standard. The truth is the potential prince finds the lifestyle of the prince overwhelming.

A good friend of mine, a prince in his own right, was dating this guy. Things were seemingly going so well that my friend introduced his new beau to his friends, only to have his new beau end their budding relationship a few days later. When my friend inquired as to why, his now former beau explained that he did not fit into the prince's circle of friends. The prince and his friends were well educated, had established careers and had investments, such as homes, stocks, bonds, and retirement funds. The former beau considered himself "unsuccessful," inadequate and mediocre. Though in the same age group, the former beau's idea of a "good time" was still clubbing, sexing everyone he could, and smoking weed daily. Rather than focusing on the prince with whom he had other commonalities, including a wonderful spiritual and physical connection, he focused on the expectations, duties, and responsibilities of the princedom and discarded the prince.

I have had the same scenario happen to me repeatedly. A former beau with whom I shared an amazing connection did not feel that he had enough education to be with me and has since returned to school. Periodically, he calls me to let me know how he is progressing. Another former beau, very attractive, almost thirty, claimed that my friends were "too professional." Yet another claimed he did not have enough in common with me and my friends; another one said he felt that he had to constantly watch what he said or did around me because of my professional standing. The irony is that after dating me, several of my former beaux have sought to become more successful. They rejected me, the prince, and my princedom because of who I was, yet they are now pursuing "success," so they can feel successful by the standards they used to critique me. Was I too much for them to handle at that time, even though

I did not pressure them to change the essence of who they were; I just wanted them to be with me? I do not care if my man is a construction worker, sanitation operator or fast food worker, as long as he is a black man with a plan...for his life... and is secure in himself and his manhood. It is not about how successful a man is, it is about that man striving to fulfill his purpose on earth.

I remember when I was a child, everyone told me that all the little girls would be after me because (1) I would be more handsome than I was already and (2) I would be successful. I am in my thirties, and I am still waiting for that to happen! As a same- gender loving man, what I now know is that the more education I have acquired and the more successful I am, the smaller the dating pool has become. When I moved to the black gay mecca of Atlanta, Georgia, I expected to meet other princes like myself who were upwardly mobile and available. Instead, I have met more "frogs" – men who do not have themselves together and do not know how to respond to those who do.

Recently, I was watching the late night recap of one of Atlanta's premier morning shows, and the host posed a question to listeners. He asked, "Would you 'date-down' – date someone who is not on the same socioeconomic level as you?" Some callers rejected the idea based on personal experiences of having done so unsuccessfully while others explained that they had successful experiences dating down. After several minutes of debate, the host concluded that dating down has the potential to work if the belle or beau in the situation could match his or her upwardly mobile suitor in (1) class, (2) etiquette, (3) exposure, (4) knowledge, and (5) spirituality.

The host first dispelled the misnomer that class has nothing to do with socioeconomic status, but rather it has everything to do with how a person carries himself or herself. I have had several guys to stop dating me because they realized that two of us were not of the same social class. What they did not perceive and understand is that I became a prince by way of working-class parents in a struggling community. I was taught by my parents and others in our community to carry myself with dignity and grace - something that used to be a staple in the African-American community, regardless of how much or how little you had. No matter what social setting you found yourself in, you could at the very least be courteous and respectfully represent your family and community in a manner which would make everyone proud. Secondly, the potential belle or beau must know how to conduct himself or herself in public – at restaurants, cultural events, dinner. I come from working-class parents, whose families were rooted and grounded in generational poverty. I had to learn that a dinner could consist of several courses. Growing up, I thought that there was one course – dinner! Let's eat! However, I learned how to behave in polite society by being exposed to banquets and balls. Thirdly, exposure to different cultures, cultural activities, and events through domestic and international travel is essential. Potential beaus and belles must at least be willing to experience or have already experienced the world outside of their local communities. One of the most shocking things one of my former beaux said to me while considering a trip to Puerto Rico with me was, "I am not never being nowhere." Fourthly, the potential beau or belle must be knowledgeable of national and international news (political events, crime, natural disasters, cultural celebrations, sporting events, etc.) and acquire knowledge through reading a variety of literature which helps to create conversation. If two involved people cannot converse about a variety of topics and issues that affect their daily lives, then how can the pair grow together? Lastly, and most important as it relates to relationship growth, is that upwardly mobile suitor and his or her potential beau or belle must be "equally yoked spiritually," worshipping the same God and in agreement concerning various aspects of religion and spirituality. After all, how can two people walk together, except they agree - headed in the same direction?

Even though this is a possible solution to "dating-down" and to the prince/beau or prince/belle problem, a quandary still exists for a prince like me. If the dating pool is smaller as a result of my perceived success and guys are not willing to "date up" even though I am willing to "date down," will I ever have the fairytale that I have dreamt of since I was a little boy?

The autopsy report stated that it was this realization that caused the death of the fairytale. I sat at the computer that day and grieved. I literally cried for the loss of something that had once been very precious to me – something that I sincerely believed in, hope for, prayed for, and patterned a portion of my life after. Sitting there

I accepted not only the possibility, but the overwhelming probability – that there would not be a "once upon a time" nor a "happily ever after" for me. As emptiness set in and I grappled with my newfound reality, I had a strange epiphany. The fairytale had died, but the prince had not. I am a prince. I am real. I have so much to offer, and I have so much love to give. The fairytale had died; however, the prince still lives; but, what is a prince without a fairytale?

QUESTIONS OF RECONCILIATION

According to the Bible, God told Adam in the garden, "It is not good for man to be alone." However, we classify ourselves, we all need and desire human companionship. Unfortunately, many of us have unrealistic expectations of relationships because we have been socialized to believe in the fairytale. Consider these questions:

Is your idea of love and relationships based upon childhood fairytales?

Do the fairytales need to die in order for you to experience a realistic love?

If it means having a sustainable relationship, are you will to "date down" and/or "date up?"

Noah's Arc:
The Restoration of Hope

As part of his birthday celebration, I took a guy whom I had dated off and on for four years to see the movie Noah's Arc: Jumping the Broom, which was actually the series finale to the cancelled TV show of the same name. I had not been a fan of the television show, for I did not have the Logo channel as a part of my cable package. The information I gathered about the show came as a result of watching an occasional episode at a friend's house or on DVD or reading an online synopsis. However, by the time the movie came out, I was abreast of all the characters and their histories. Therefore, I was excited to see this movie, which was being shown at a small independent theater in midtown Atlanta.

I expected the movie to be as entertaining as the TV series, but I did not expect the movie to have such a profound impact on me. From the moment, the camera panned from behind Noah, fashionably dressed, with his leather riding boats propped against the rail of the ferry headed toward Martha's Vineyard, to the closing shot of Noah and Wade dancing at their post nuptial celebration, I cried.... like a newborn baby...I cried...like the Young and the Restless' Nikki; I cried like The Bold and the Beautiful Brooke; I cried... to the point that my entire face was wet and tear stained. Though I tried to conceal my tears, it did not work. I felt the eyes of my date and many others around me looking at me as if I had lost my mind. It was not until after the credits had rolled, and we had exited the theater that I began to analyze why I had such a strong emotional reaction to this "story," to this "work of fiction," to this tale from the imaginative mind of the show's creator and writer. These "people" were not real! They were nothing more than characters in a convoluted portrayal of gay life. It was fiction! Fiction! Fiction! Fiction! Right? Then why did I cry? I cried for several reasons – none of which I could fully articulate until weeks later.

Noah's Arc: Jumping the Broom was not art imitating life; I finally realized that the stories of each one of the principal characters represented pages out of my own life and the lives of others I knew. After further reflection, I concluded that there were three reasons for my emotional meltdown. First, I was overwhelmed by the mere fact that I was in a public theater, watching a movie in which all of the principal characters were gay African-American males, without any fear whatsoever. I live in Atlanta, Georgia, a mecca for not only heterosexual socially upwardly mobile African-Americans, but for same-gender loving African-Americans as well. To sit in a theater full of same-gender loving African-American males, whom I am certain were all touched by this movie, even if not to the extent I was, because Noah's Arc was symbolic of their arc – personal stories coming to life – the experience was absolutely liberating and validating! The TV series and the movie celebrated US as human beings with unrecognized expressions and invalidated experiences. It was not art imitating life – it was just life – our lives, our moments. Finally, this movie (as well as the TV series) portrayed gay African-American males in a relatively positively light. It gave voice to the marginalized, giving us a voice and platform from which to be heard. Noah's Arc was not just a TV series and a movie – it was our voice!

Secondly, I cried because the movie is relevant to what is happening now in our society. This movie deals with events surroundings Noah and Wade's wedding weekend at Martha's Vineyard in Massachusetts. The subject of gay marriage in American society has been a heated issue over the last decade. The whole notion of marriage defined as a union between a man and woman was the platform which led to the re-election of George Bush in 2004. Even the first-ever elected Black President Barack Obama has taken a somewhat laissez-faire approach to the issue of same-sex marriage. Nevertheless, in spite of the opposition of many right-winged Republicans, Democrats and fundamental Christians, gay marriage is slowly becoming a glaring reality in American society. In fact, the movie Noah's Arc is set in Massachusetts, the first state to legalize same-sex marriages on November 18, 2003. Since then, Connecticut, Iowa, Vermont, Maine, New Hampshire, and California have paved the way, recognizing that homosexuals are entitled to marriage and marital benefits, just like heterosexuals. Other states are moving toward recognizing domestic partnerships and civil unions. The Noah's Arc movie clearly communicates that gay marriage is a possible for those of us in the African-American community, who long to take our loving and committed relationships to a more permanent and stable level through legal unions or marriages. Again, the movie validated our right to exist - our right to life, liberty, and the pursuit of happiness – unalienable rights endowed to us by Our Creator but denied to us by man. It validates our right to our version of the American Dream which our families, churches, communities and country refuse to respect. It validates the way that we love and express ourselves which American society has boasted "ain't Civil and ain't Rights."

Noah's Arc paid homage to our slave heritage. The subtitle of this movie is Jumping the Broom. A brief history lesson: During slavery, American slaves were considered more property than personage. As a result, African slaves did not have civil or human rights which included the right to marry without the permission of their owners. Unable to express their commitment legally, slaves expressed their commitment symbolically – in the only manner they knew and could. Jumping the broom became an outward symbol of an inward commitment. If two slaves wanted to marry, a plantation minister or a respected elder (male or female) would perform the ritual, and the couple would literally "jump the broom" and be married in the eyes of the plantation community. Noah and Wade repeated this ritual at the end of their wedding ceremony. Just as society did not recognize the personage and civil rights of African- American slaves, society today fails to recognize the personage and civil rights of the same-gender loving community. I find it ironic that many African-Americans side with the oppressor (white America) in denying homosexuals civil rights. How dare we! How dare African- Americans label homosexuals as "queer" when we of African descent are still considered "queer," "savages," "barbarians," and "sexually deviant" by our oppressors. Seeing the custom of "jumping the broom" depicted in this movie solidified my position that gay marriage has nothing to do with whether or not God created "Adam for Eve" or "Adam for Steve" (He actually created both). On the contrary, it is having everything to do with equality and equity under the law in American society. Even though I am a same-gender loving African-American male, I still grew up desiring the "American Dream." Who has the right to tell me that my version of the "American Dream" is wrong? After all, it is my dream.

Again...I cried...I cried for joy because Noah's Arc restored my personal dream – the hope that I too could experience a love so deep and abiding that I would be unashamed of it...just like Noah and Wade. Wade was willing to turn away his own mother, a pastor's wife, from the ceremony if she showed disapproval or disrespect toward his husband.

I cried because I knew that, without a shadow of a doubt, I could not settle for a love that was anything less than I desired or deserved. I cried because, after feeling ashamed of who and what I was for years, I now own me... I cried for all of these reasons – the once impossible is now possible: openness, acceptance, relationship, companionship, and yes – marriage! I cried simply because Noah's Arc restored my hope.

Questions of Reconciliation

Our world is changing. More and more, homosexuality is becoming socially acceptable. Same-sex marriage is no longer a possibility, but a reality that will alter religious and secular society. Consider these questions:

As a same-gender loving man, do you view the homosexual lifestyle as legitimate?

Is the same-sex marriage issue purely a civil dispute, religious dispute, or both or perhaps a moral issue?

Are you open to the possibility of marrying your same-sex partner?

What are the possible benefits or determents of doing so?

REAL MAN:
DEFINED AND PERSONIFIED

I grew up in the Baptist church. After I left the Baptist church, I joined a Pentecostal church and more than a year later I had the Pentecostal experience – the Baptism of the Holy Spirit with the signs of speaking in tongues as the Spirit of God gave utterance through me or my voice as evidenced in the Book of Acts 2:1. The church in which I had this phenomenal experience was really progressive and on the "cutting edge" of urban church ministry. In this particular church, God was allowed to be God, moving by His might, power, and spirit. God's presence was welcomed, and I literally saw first century church ministry occur: the lame was made to walk, the blinded eyes were opened, demons and devils were cast out, and prophecy went in addition to many other signs and wonders. What also made this church unique was that it had a large number of closeted African-American same gender loving (SGL) congregants who served in every capacity in the church from the pulpit to the backdoor. I was one of those members…

As phenomenal, dynamic, and "invisibly inclusive" as this church was, it was still traditional in every sense of the word. Homosexuality and homosexuals were merely "tolerated" and not "celebrated" or respected. Although my pastor did his best to promote that homosexuals and heterosexuals are all the same at the foot of Calvary's cross (although true), his personal disdain for homosexuality still came across the pulpit. I believe that he genuinely loved the same-gender loving members of his flock; however, he did not see homosexual males as real men. Often times during our highly spiritual, emotional Sunday and Wednesday services, men experiencing relief from natural and spiritual forces of oppression came to the altar. Whenever a male, especially one whose sexuality was in question, was ministered to, the pastor would call for the real men to come and encourage him. In droves, real men – heterosexual members - would come from all over the sanctuary, embracing and encouraging this "broken brother" while we, the same-gender loving male congregants, stood in shameful supportive silence, our souls stinging from the overt pastoral diss. It was during one of these services that I asked myself the question, "What is a real man?"

By secular and religious standards, many people define a real man as a male who is first and foremost heterosexual and masculine. He is rough and rugged and likes masculine things like women, cars, and sports. He has that "machismo," that "thug- appeal," that "swagga." However, a real man is employable and employed. If not educated, he has skills that can bring gainful employment so that he can support himself and his family. He does not rely on anyone – his parents or his woman. He is a real man – self-sufficient. He takes care of the women in his life – whether his wife, mother, sister, daughter, or niece. If he has children, he provides for them; their needs come before his own. He leaves a legacy for them to continue. A real man cries and is not afraid to express his emotions in public or in private; he does not let his "swagga" or "machismo" get in his way. Most importantly, a real man loves God; he is aware of the Christ consciousness within himself, in others, and in the world.

Many, especially in the African-American church and Christendom in general, would argue that these are all exceptional qualities of a real man. However, in our community, any man, no matter how phenomenal he is, would be discredited as a real man if he has effeminate qualities or is openly same-gender loving. In the twenty-first century, many people still equate masculinity and heterosexuality with the concept of a real man. A real man can be unemployable or unemployed, delinquent in child support, living off his woman (mother, daughter, or niece), disrespectful, emotionless, worse than an infidel and still be labeled a real man simply because he is heterosexual and masculine. However, the exact opposite is true for a homosexual male. He does not have to be effeminate; he can be as masculine as men come, but if he shares his bed with another man and has or does ninety-nine percent of the aforementioned characteristics exceptionally well, he is a sissy – nothing more, nothing less! Sunday after Sunday, Wednesday after Wednesday, I as well as the entire congregation and the other same-gender loving male congregants, whether overtly gay, on the DL, or completely closeted, were inadvertently sent a message that we were not good enough – we were not real men.

"Manhood" is too often equated with "maleness." A male is classified as a male simply because he has a penis and a scrotum. However, just because one is classified as such, does not make a male a man. A male is no more a man due to his anatomical structure than he is simply because he can reproduce offspring. Yet, this is how society still qualifies and designates manhood. In the African-American community, some men have a tendency to brag about and are praised for the number of children they have; however, how many in the African-American community question whether or not these men are financially and emotionally supporting their offspring? We have heard the old cliché – that still rings true –any man can produce a baby, but it takes a real man to raise a child.

When African-American heterosexual men are not parenting their offspring, then who is helping single mothers raise their children? More than we care acknowledge in the African-American community, same-gender-loving African-American males are stepping up to the plate and are directly and indirectly shaping black boys into real African-American men, instilling in them a sense of self-worth and love for their families and communities. In spite of all the good that same-gender-loving African-American males continue to do in churches and communities, many people are still believing that if a male child is mentored, fathered, or simply comes in contact with same-gender-loving men, then that male child will be molested, sodomized, and destined to be homosexual.

As a same-gender-loving African-American male, who has taught in elementary and secondary schools, I have mentored and "fathered" many young boys who have grown up to become exceptional real men – some of which to this day call me "Dad" or "Pops." I am not sure if they knew or suspected that I was/am a same-gender-loving man; however, it does not negate the positive influence I had and still have on their lives. Many of these young men credit me with inspiring them to become upstanding or outstanding sons, husbands, fathers, and community leaders. The positive influence that I have had on the lives of boys who became men, started with my little brother who is almost thirteen years younger than I. After giving birth to my little brother, my mother went back to working nights, leaving my father and me to take care of this little bundle of joy. During the first three months of his life, my father provided most of the care during those hours that my mother was at work; however, as my brother aged, the care-giving shifted to me. As an eighth grade student, I remember sitting at the kitchen table holding him in my right arm with a pencil in my left hand, doing my homework. During the summer month when school was not in session, I was his primary care provider. I putty- trained him, taught him his letters and numbers, and provided him with the most essential love, care, and support during his formative years. As he got older, I disciplined him if he performed poorly in school, encouraged him when he became discouraged (for example, when he was not selected to the school basketball team), and did many other things that a big brother, a father-figure, and a mentor does for a young male under his care. Yet, as a same-gender-loving man, I and countless others are discounted, disqualified, and disregarded as real men because each of us shares his bed with another man.

I and many other marginalized same-gender-loving African- American men are living proof that one's manhood is not contingent upon sexuality; it is contingent upon our ability to maintain our sanity when those closest to us have discredited us as men; it is contingent upon our ability to remain confident in who we are, whether we choose to wear a pair of Tombs or a pair of six- inch stilettos. It is contingent upon our ability to achieve our goals in spite of life's adversities and to navigate between two worlds that cause us to question our identity and God's unconditional love for us; it is contingent upon our ability to father, mentor, and support our families and communities financially, spiritually, and emotionally.

Reflecting upon American history and my life experiences, I ask this question and I challenge you – whether heterosexual or homosexual - to ask this question: When will marginalized same-gender-loving African-American men be counted among the real men and stop being considered "queers" and "sexually deviants," especially by the African-American community? It was not that long ago that all African-Americans were considered "sexually deviant" and "immoral" by the dominant Anglo culture. For the better part of a hundred years, African-Americans were considered three-fifths of a person and denied the democratic rights to life, liberty, and the pursuit of happiness. Yet, same-gender-loving African-American males are not even considered to be three-fifths of a man by their own community. Has our community forgotten what it is like to be a marginalized group, fighting for basic civil rights? Have African-Americans, the once and still oppressed, become the oppressors? God forbid!

QUESTIONS OF RECONCILIATION

How we see ourselves correlates with whether or not we have or will develop a healthy self-efficacy of ourselves and how we see others. My perceptions of manhood were marred due to others' exceptions of me. Consider these questions:

How do you classify yourself: gay, bisexual, straight but likes to "mess" around, discrete, closeted, etc.?

How does your self-image/classification affect your understanding or perception of manhood?

Is there a need for you to reconcile your definition of manhood and your life/behavior?

What can openly-gay African-American same-gender-loving men do to make sure our voices respected or appreciated in our churches and in our communities?

Strange Encounters
of the Drag Kind

I got on the train at my usual stop and hastily sat in the seats closest to the door; I sat down to finish up the last few lines to an article I was writing. As soon as I glanced up, I noticed two "ladies" staring at me. Immediately, I lowered my head. As the images of the ladies registered in my mind, I realized that these were not your typical "ladies." In fact, they were not "ladies" in the traditional sense at all. They were drag queens – men dressed as women. As I continued to look down at my composition book, pretending to proofread what I had just written, I could feel the eyes of one drag queen staring at me; apparently, he was intrigued by me. As he continued to look at me, he resumed his conversation with his girlfriend. At the very moment they were chuckling about something, I became inspired to include a story in this book about transformative experiences with transgender individuals. My sudden inspiration brought a smile to my face which created a segue for the smitten queen to say something to me. "Did you hear that?" she asked seductively perhaps thinking that I was now eavesdropping on their conversation.

"No, I was thinking about something else," I replied. I couldn't let on that they had suddenly become the source of my inspiration.

I thought that would be the end of the attempt at conversation until she asked me yet another question, "Did anyone ever tell you that you look like Maxwell?"

Grinning and blushing, I replied, "Yes," thinking of one of my former students who called me by the moniker of the popular R& B singer rather than by my name.

The queen noticed that I was blushing and smiling, which led her to say, "You're cute!"

I said, "Thank you." She and her friend then went back to their conversation and I went on pretending to proofread my article, though I was actually eavesdropping on their conversation.

My admirer then began to talk about an illegal scheme (known as a "stunt" in the black gay world) that one of her his cousins pulled whom I deduced from the conversation was a transsexual too. Using a fake name and identification, her cousin ordered a house full of furniture from Rent-A-Center for her new two-bedroom apartment and scheduled it for delivery. However, the place the furniture was going to be delivered to was not her new apartment; it was a vacant apartment in an adjacent building in the same apartment complex in which she lived. Somehow, unbeknownst to my admirer, her cousin had gained access to an empty apartment to execute the scam. The delivery men – unaware of the scheme - delivered the furniture. No sooner than they left, the "stunt-queen" had some friends, who were lying in wait to move the furniture to her actual apartment. With fake identification and a false address, the queen's cousin successfully duped Rent-A-Center out of thousands of dollars in furniture and appliances since there was no way for them to track her or the stolen furniture. Incredibly smart or incredibly stupid, I do not know; however, by the conclusion of my admirer's story, I arrived at my stop. As I exited the train I said a cordial, "Have a nice day." She smiled and replied, "You too," more seductively than before. I looked back at the train as I was going up the escalator, and she was looking out of the window watching me as the train pulled off.

This open exchange was a monumental experience for me. For many years, I was afraid of "them" – drag queens. I viewed them in same manner as many of my heterosexual counterparts - freaks of nature, Frankenstein's in wigs, dresses, make up, and stilettos. This experience took me back to my first encounter with the world of drag when I was a freshman in college. I was nineteen years old and very new to the gay life, even though I had been aware of my sexuality since I was about four years old. My boyfriend and I went to one of the only African-American gay clubs in Memphis called "X- scape." It was fitting name for it, offering the African-American gay and bisexual men in the city an escape from the pretense that was our lives. It was an escape from my faux heterosexuality to my gay reality – a reality that I was still in many ways unwilling to accept.

We arrived at the club just as the line-up for the drag show was about to be announced. We hurriedly found a table and sat down near the front of the stage. I leaned over to my boyfriend and asked, "What's a drag show?" He looked at me in disbelief. Even though he was only a few months older than I, he had been "out" since he was fifteen years old. In my opinion, he was an "expert" in all things gay. He explained what a drag show was by first defining the term "drag queen." I was like, "O.K." I wasn't totally naïve; I had seen men dressed as women, but never before had I been this up-close and personal to them.

The drag show began, and the little dingy hole-in-the-wall transformed into a Broadway stage with lights and costumes. The music started and the first drag queen hit the stage.... much to my surprise wearing next to NOTHING! Somehow she managed to cover her "pe-gina" with dollar bills. I was so shocked at the dollar bills covering "pe-gina" that it took me a moment to notice that she had breast too! I wasn't sure I was seeing things correctly! I leaned over to my boyfriend and asked, "Are those what I think they are?" I gazed at her chest.

"Yes!" he replied. "Are they real?" He did not reply; he just looked at me and rolled his eyes. I took that as a yes. As the drag queen performed, I looked her over from the crown of her head to the soles of her six- inch stilettos. I stared at this chocolate brown god-dess; she had the smoothest skin I had seen on a woman or a man. Her hair – I don't think it was weave – was long, flowing, and honey blond. I was so taken by her appearance that I do not remember what song she performed;

all I remember was her nakedness…breast-ta-ses…and pegina.

After she exited the stage, another drag queen was introduced. Unlike the first, she was clothed. More than being clothed, she was tastefully and eloquently dressed in shimmering flowing sequined gown that resembled one Whitney Houston wore in the movie The Bodyguard when she performed "I Have Nothing." However, this lady did not lip-sync the Whitney song; she performed Toni Braxton's "Seven Whole Days" and electrified the crowd. I was even impressed and gave her a standing ovation along with the rest of the club. My boyfriend went a step further and gave her a tip. After her performance, I just sat there in disbelief that a man dressed as a woman with such poise and grace could do…. that! Amazing…absolutely amazing! Just as the pendulum had swung from horror to amazement, it soon swung back over to horror again…

A few minutes later, this same drag queen returned for her second performance. This time she was not as flamboyantly dressed; she was dressed in a sequined evening gown suitable for a church banquet. I fully expected her to arouse the crowd again with another popular song; perhaps, this time she would do a Whitney Houston number. Instead of performing a song by Whitney, Toni, Anita, or any other R&B or pop diva of the day, she performed renowned Gospel artist Milton Brunson and the Thompson Community Choir's "There is No Failure in God." I couldn't believe my ears! Is she serious? Surely, she wasn't doing a gospel song in a gay club? My face contorted as I sat there wondering what in the hell was going on. The crowd, including my God-fearing, church hopping boyfriend, and two friends, who had come with us, enthusiastically clapped and sang with her. I looked at everyone around me internally asking, Are they crazy? I questioned their fear, respect, and reverence for God. Have they no shame? Then, to add insult to injury, after she finished that song, she followed up with another gospel song - "Stand Up" by O'landa Draper and the Associates.

> *Stand up for right*
> *Join in the fight*
> *Be a soldier for Jesus*

To make this abominable experience even more abominable, a club punk, this fat queen, had the nerve to shout "Hallelujah" and "Thank you, Jesus," and even danced around the club as if he was at a Holy Ghost tent revival.

Awed yet unimpressed, I sat there with my mouth wide open! I couldn't believe what I was experiencing. In the midst of this club - this escape - this man had the nerve, the audacity, the unmitigated gall to perform not one – but two gospel songs. How dare he mix the secular and the sacred! How dare he/she/it invite Christ where he did not go...to the X-scape! Outraged, I told my boyfriend we were leaving and I stormed out. Once I sped off the parking lot on two wheels, I lit into him for subjecting me to such sacrilege. His response to me and our friends was, "Don't mess with him and *his* Jesus!" As if, I had a monopoly on the Christ...

Somewhere in my nineteen-year-old inexperienced, self- righteous mind, I agreed with him. Jesus was mine. It was one thing to struggle with homosexuality, but it was something totally different to don yourself in women's apparel with augmented body parts, and prance across a stage performing gospel songs as if God was pleased with your life? Spare me! How could you perform such a song that says "stand up for right" when everything you are doing is so wrong! Again, it was one thing to struggle with my own homosexuality, but I thought that his being a gospel singing drag queen was beyond redemption and a sure fire ticket to hell!

For many years my disdain for drag queens was based solely upon my experience that night. That night added to my confusion about the whole gay lifestyle. It was just too much for me to handle. As a result of that and other occurrences, I soon dumped my boyfriend, then retreated more into the church, and renounced my homosexuality. After eight years of self-righteousness and sexual suppression, I had come full circle dealing with my sexuality. In doing so, I picked up right where I had left off with many things and many people, including my position or feelings about drag queens! It was eight years later that I encountered another drag queen. By this time, I was living in Atlanta, Georgia, because I wanted to move beyond the spiritual and geographic limitations of my hometown. Atlanta seemed to be a progressive and liberal city in the midst of the deep, traditional South. This physical move or shift was in line with what was already occurring within me. My religious paradigm was shifting – changing- and it was a change I welcomed.

One Monday night, my boyfriend – a different one from eight years earlier- and I decided to go to this new comedy club located right up the street from where we lived. Clubs in the Atlanta area often designate one or more nights to cater to the city's homosexual demographic. Mondays at this newly-opened club featured performances by homosexual comedians and drag queens. Consequently, in an attempt to step outside my box, I went to this comedy club. The emcee for that night was a local celebrity drag queen who later became a local radio personality. She was not like the queens I had seen some years earlier; she was not glamorously made-up in the image of some diva nor was she arrayed in spectacular costumes. She was as ugly as homemade sin; her costume was an old woman's gray wig and a house dress similar to ones found in my grandmother's closet. Her repertoire of songs included nothing secular – only Gospel songs. Her signature lip- sync was "Jesus Can Work It Out" by Father Hayes and the Cosmopolitan Church Choir.

When the D.J. began to play that track and she stepped out on stage, I said to myself, History is repeating itself! Once again, I sat there flabbergasted. As people walked to the stage from their seats to give her tips, I watched in pure amazement as I had done some eight years earlier, wondering, "What is it with drag queens? Why do they insist on mixing the sacred and the secular? Rather than storming out in self-righteous indignation as I had done eight years earlier, I stayed because this time I knew and understood that there was a lesson God was trying to teach me. After her musical performance, she went straight into her comedic routine. I was surprised! She was genuinely funny! She had the crowd in stitches; I was actually sitting in the midst of a drag queen – the likes of which I previously had found utterly repulsive – having a great time! The most memorable moment occurred when my cell phone rang in the middle of her comedy routine. She stopped and walked over to my table as if to say, "No, your phone didn't ring in the middle of my show." I became frightened because I did not know what she was going to do next; I feared for my life, for I had heard a long time ago that you didn't want to mess with drag queens because they would wind-mill you to death! My heart was beating fast as I scrambled to silence my phone. She looked at me! I looked at her! Everyone, including my boyfriend, was looking at us and laughing. I silenced the phone. Without causing me further embarrassment, she walked away from the table and continued her routine as if my cell phone had not interrupted the show. After the awkward moment, I laughed because what had happened was truly hilarious! Somewhere in the midst of my laughter, a seed was planted – one that would grow and eventually change my perception of drag queens...

Several years later, after the dissolution of my relationship with my boyfriend with whom I had moved to Atlanta, I began dating this handsome guy who shared a house with several of his friends. One evening when I picked him up for a date, I had the privilege of meeting Josh, one of his roommates. While my date finished dressing, I chatted with Josh in the living room. I found out that Josh and I had a lot in common. He was a former elementary school teacher, who quit to start his own entertainment company and had been really successfully. I applauded him for following his dreams! We even talked about love and relationships and how difficult it is to find a good man in Atlanta. (Yes, he was gay too!) I concurred; it was over these likenesses that we bonded. He lamented over past relationships and hurt; I could tell that he struggled with loneliness and deeply desire to have a significant other. A few minutes later, my date was ready and we left.

In the car, I told my guy about the wonderful conversation that Josh and I had and how I admired Josh for following in his dreams. He seemed surprised that I had taken a liking to Josh. He asked me a couple questions: "Did he tell you what type of entertainment business he runs?"

"No!" When Josh said he was in the "entertainment business," I assumed that he was some type of club promoter or a manager who helped undiscovered talent break into the music business; after all, Atlanta is known as a city where many artists have been discovered. My date then told me Josh managed some gay male strippers and that three of his roommates were Josh's clients. With surprise and shock in my voice, I said, "Oh!" I was shocked, but then again, I wasn't. After all, I left the self-righteous, judgmental super-saint that I had been back in Memphis.

My guy chuckled at my response and then asked: Did Josh tell you what he does?

I replied, "Yeah," as if asking him, Didn't you just tell me that he manages strippers?

My date said, "No, not just that, he does something else as well. "What?" I asked wondering what in the world he was referring to

He then revealed, "Josh has an "alter-ego" whose name is Jewell. "An alter-ego?" I repeated not comprehending what he was talking about.

"Yes, an alter-ego." He looked at me hoping that I would catch on or that I knew what he was talking about. I will be the first to admit that sometimes I cannot see the forest for the trees. After a few seconds of my not getting what he was hinting at, my guy said it in a way I was sure to understand. "He's a drag queen! A tranny!"

I almost wrecked my car! "What!" I exclaimed. "A drag queen?"

My date laughed because he knew that I did not have a clue prior to that moment. My date further explained that the somewhat homely Josh, with whom I had had this wonderful bonding session transformed into the comely, radiant, and effervescent Jewell in makeup, heels, a wig, and a dress that sparkled! She became witty, outgoing, and an absolute crowd pleaser when performing. The excitement in my guy's voice when he spoke about Jewell even intrigued me.

I then reflected on or reviewed my conversation with Josh. It was obvious that he was gay. He wasn't the most masculine man in the world, but that's not uncommon...especially in Atlanta. I am not the most masculine guy in the world! He was at the house in sweats, sitting and watching TV alone as I have done on so many occasions. I went over every detail I could remember of the time I spent in his presence, remembering his physical appearance and our conversation, looking for signs that he was a drag queen. I remembered that his eyebrows were arched, but who doesn't arch his/her eyebrows today? I remembered that he had no facial hair whatsoever, but then I thought about me. I didn't have any facial hair, and I wasn't a drag queen.

Perhaps I didn't see signs of a drag queen because that's not what I was supposed to see. I was simply supposed to see a human being someone with whom I had common interests, whether he was in sweats or a full length evening gown. In that moment, I learned how to see Josh as God sees us all. Whereas "man looks at the outward appearance . . . the Lord looks at the heart" (I Samuel 16:7 NIV). The revelation that Josh transformed into Jewell did not change the fact that we had bonded over like interests. I was learning to look beyond the outward appearance whether that appearance is bisexual, gay, lesbian, transgendered, or straight – and look at the heart and soul of a person. We are all more alike than we are different with similar (if not identical) life experiences in one respect or another. From that night forward, whether I walked in the door and saw Josh or Jewell, he or she had my utmost respect as a human being and a child of God, for in God, "there is neither Jew nor Greek, slave nor free, male or female" (Galatians 3:28). He loves us all. Now I understand why those two drag queens in a gay club could boldly proclaim that "There Is No Failure in God" and encourage us all to "Stand Up for Right" and testify that "Jesus Can Work It Out" and then turn around and heal our souls with the medicine of laughter. We are all the same at the foot of the cross! No one – regardless of how holy and righteous you think you are, no matter how hard you fast and pray, no matter how long you lay prostrate before the Lord, no matter how fluent your tongues, no matter how well you preach and prophesy – no one has a monopoly on the Christ.

QUESTIONS OF RECONCILIATION

Even though I struggled because I was a same-gender loving man, condemned to hell by Christian teachings, I was still self-righteous and looked down upon other same-gender loving individuals – transsexuals, transgendered, etc., without recognizing that just as I am, they too are children of God. Consider these questions:

How do you view drag queens (transsexual or transgendered men)?

Do you think a transsexual or a transgender man is more or less of a man by your standards of manhood?

Do you believe that transsexual or transgendered individuals have a place in God's family? Elaborate on your response.

What role, if any, do you think gender assignment plays in God's plan for his children?

I Am Not My Hair:
Loc-ing A New Identity

Little girl with the press and curl
Age eight I got a Jheri curl
Thirteen then I got a relaxer
I was a source of so much laughter
Fifteen when it all broke off
Eighteen and then I went all natural
February two thousand and two
I Went and did what I had to do
Cause it was time to change my life
To become the woman that I am inside
Ninety-seven dreadlocks all gone
Looked in the mirror for the first time and saw
that Hey...
I am not my hair
I am not this skin
I am not your ex-pec-tations no
I am not my hair
I am not this skin
I am a soul that lives within

-India.Arie

The aforementioned lyrics is an exert from one of my favorite songs, "I Am Not My Hair," by Grammy award-winning neo-soul artist India Arie. I first heard this song late one night while watching the Tom Joyner Show on TV One. Upon hearing the very first verse of the song, I immediately identified with its message, for just like India Arie, I had identity struggles directly related to my hair. I have always loved my hair, even as a toddler. Once I adamantly resisted getting my hair cut, which resulted in my mother whipping me with the razor strap on the side of the barber's chair. According to dominant cultural standards of beauty and excellence that have been erroneously forced upon the African-Americans, I do not have the best grade or texture of hair. In fact, my hair is quite course, making it difficult to comb. It is for this reason that my parents, especially mother, insisted that I have a weekly haircut. The instructions to the barber were always the same – cut it as low as possible. I hated low haircuts; I have an oddly shaped head which is magnified with the absence of hair. However, throughout my elementary and junior high years, I was subjected to the will of my parents until I became of the age when I began to care more about my appearance. Even then, my mother required that I maintain my hair. "If you don't keep it up, you are getting it all cut off!" I accepted this condition, and from junior high school throughout high school, I was allowed some liberality with my hairstyle choices. I experimented with everything from the Gumby to the processed S-Curl to the high top fade made infamous by Christopher "Kid" Reid of the hip-hop duo Kid-N-Play. By the time I was a freshman in college, I was contemplating dying my hair a light shade of brown – an idea that was quickly shot down by two powerful entities in my life: my mother and my church!

I think my mother thought that it would make me look "gay!" Since I had renounced my "gaydom," I did not want to do anything else that would bring unwanted attention to me. By that time, I had experimented with the gay lifestyle and was now trying to distance myself from it. One of the ways I did that was by throwing myself headfirst into my church in hopes of cleansing my "sin-sick" soul. I felt my homosexual experimentation had sullied my earthly and heavenly reputation. Therefore, the only way I could redeem myself was through repentance and sanctification. I had been taught to "come out from among them and be ye separate" (1 Corinthians 6:17). To live a holy life was to live a separate life and not indulge (let alone enjoy) worldly pleasures. Sanctification also meant being modest in dress and appearance and not "looking like the world." Therefore, my dyed light-brown hair would not have been acceptable for someone of my caliber – an aspiring church leader. As a result, I conformed to the expectations of my church and my pastor for whom I had (and still have) a great deal of respect and admiration. For several years, I wore a very conservative hairstyle – a low fade. However, as my spiritual paradigm began to shift, my hair began to grow, and before I knew it, I was sporting a baby afro. I literally loved my hair and I always kept it neatly groomed. Even though I loved my baby afro, I soon learned that my pastor did not...

One night after Bible study, a fellow young minister and afro- wearing friend and I were called into a meeting by the president of the ministerial alliance. He promptly told us that our hairstyles were not becoming of young ministers; therefore, we needed to cut off our baby afros and go for something more conservative. My friend and I looked at each other in disbelief and then he indignantly asked the following questions: "What does our hair have to do with our ability to serve the people of this congregation? Are we not faithful to God and this church? Are we not consistent in our giving and attendance?" The ministerial alliance president could only answer my colleague's question in the affirmative, but he was adamant; we needed to cut our hair. I understood that that mandate was actually not from him; it was from our pastor. My colleague flat out refused to cut his hair. The ministerial president then made us aware of the consequences if we did not conform to the expectations of our pastor: "If you do not cut your hair, you will not be allowed to serve as a part of the ministerial staff; you will be sat down." With that ultimatum, the president exited the room. My colleague was irate. So was I, but rather than be brash by absolutely refusing to change my hair, I decided to approach the situation diplomatically. Until recently, I had served as one of my pastor's adjutants. I was his personal servant; wherever he went, I was sure to follow (whether civic events or preaching engagements, etc.) Therefore, I knew how to get his attention.

The very next night, he and the church were invited to another church to celebrate the anniversary of the pastor and his wife. My pastor was to preach and the other auxiliaries were to, including me! My pissed-off colleague chose not to attend the service, but I was there on time and ready to serve. However, my demeanor was different! I was unusually quiet, and my pastor noticed this as he was preaching. Rather than giving an "Amen" or a "Hallelujah" in support of what he was saying, I sat there in silence. I didn't move a muscle! I wanted him to know that I was angry and troubled by his request. All of my life, I had been told what to do and what not to do with my hair by parents, and now my pastor wanted to do the same? My colleague was right! What did our hair have to do with our ability to serve the people? What did our hair have to do with our faithfulness to God and the church? What did our hair have to do with our giving and attendance? Surely, I was not taking my tithe to pay for my haircut or skipping church to get a haircut! This situation was more than just about hair. It was about growth! My paradigm was shifting, and I was beginning to come to terms with me, my sexuality, and my spirituality. I couldn't cut my hair! To do so would impede my growth and my development. I was starting to come into my own personage – aside from the expectations of my family and my church. There was no way in hell I was turning back now!

After the service, just as we were about to get into our cars and leave, I had a private conversation with my pastor. I told him about the meeting that my colleague and I had had with the ministerial alliance president the night before and that we both understood his request. I offered a compromise... I showed up at church with a slightly different look. My sides were more tapered and my baby afro was an inch and a half lower, but nevertheless it was still intact. It was lower and neater; it was a compromise, but it was not the total surrender that my pastor had mandated! He looked at my hair and decided that the height of it was something he could comfortably accept. I continued to be faithful to God and to serve him and the church as I had been doing until God released me to move to Atlanta the following year. I left with the blessings of my pastor, the church, and with my baby afro that was bigger than it had been before I had been mandated to cut it.

Upon moving to Atlanta, my hair continued to grow and my paradigm continued to shift. For the first time in my life, I began to see God in a way that I had never experienced him before, and I began to blossom as a person. My baby afro soon plateaued, and I decided that I needed to do something else with my hair. Cutting it was out of the question because I loved the experience and the natural and spiritual growth that I associated with it. One day, while webcaming with this guy I met online, I complimented him on his hair. He was a handsome, chocolate brother with a nicely toned physique and with long locks falling down his back. I told him that I was looking to do something different with my hair and before I knew it, he gave me the name and number of his stylist and told me that she specialized in natural hair. That day was the first and last time this brother and I ever spoke; however, the impression and suggestion he made caused me to make a decision about my hair; I decided to lock my hair. At the time I did not know anything about locs. My knowledge was limited to T.C. Carson, who sported locs on the television show Living Single and to my barber back home who had heavy locs that cascaded down his back. I remember a conversation we had about hair and how there is strength in it. He once asked me, "Have you noticed that our hair [people of African descent] grows toward the sun?"

No, I had not noticed it, but I was more apt to belief there was strength in the hair since such was mentioned in the story of "Sampson and Delilah" from the Bible. I considered the idea of loc- ing... Whether there is strength in the hair or any significance in the fact that the hair of people of African descent grows toward the sun, I did not know, but one thing I did know was that if I chose to loc my hair, it would be stark departure from the conservative, sanctified, Pentecostal image that I had careful crafted over the years. I also understand stood that it would be a major step in embracing a new identity – one in which my sexuality and my spirituality were reconciled. With that revelation at the forefront of my mind, I made the decision that I was ready to take the next step in the shaping of my new identity. I called the stylist and made an appointment for a consultation for the following day.

The consultation was to discuss the process and to determine if I even had enough hair to start it. The consultation with the stylist went very well. She thoroughly explained the process and told me that she thought that locs would look great on me. I was convinced more than ever that this was something I wanted to do. I made an appointment for that Thursday after work. Upon making the appointment, I became extremely nervous. Oh my God! I am actually going to do this! I thought! What will my family and friends think?!?! I worried! Then I thought again! It does not matter what they think! This is about me and my growth and development! I decided not to tell my family. They would see my hair when they came to visit the following the month. The only people I told were my best friend (who was not in favor of it, but still very supportive) and one of my colleagues (who was considering the same).

The next day after work, I returned to the shop. By the time I arrived, the stylist was ready for me. She washed my massive afro first and then took me to her station. I sat there literally quivering. I thought to myself, this is what change feels like! As she began to twist my hair using natural gel and a comb, I knew that I would never be the same. I knew that my old identity – one that

I had created out of fear and damnation, one that was primarily based upon everyone's expectations of me, instead of the expectations I had for myself – was dying! I knew that a new identity – one that would be inclusive of everything I am - was being birthed! After two hours of labor pains (I am very tender-headed; having my hair twisted using a small comb was excruciatingly painful for me), I looked in the mirror for the first time and saw that, *Hey... I am not my hair, I am not this skin, I am not your ex-pectations. No no, I am not my hair, I am not this skin, I am a soul that lives within...*

Questions of Reconciliation

Through my hair, my identity was shaped and controlled by others until I gained enough strength and courage to defy their expectations. Consider these questions:

What persons have helped to shape your identity – positively or negatively?

What experiences have shaped your identity? Is this current identity one you have shaped or one that has been shaped for you?

What can you do to discover or recover your identity?

Now that you are changing, what challenges have you faced or do you believe you will face?

I woke up! And I knew that it was time. After years of open silence, I knew the time had come for me to tell my father I was gay. I confirmed what my mother already knew when I was nineteen years old, but I had never formally and officially told my daddy. The reason was simple: I was closer to my mother. There is no denying that I am "Mama's baby." My mama was the more supportive one who pushed me and was at every school program and parent-teacher conference. My mama was the one who could "make a way out of no way" when it came to providing the things that I needed and wanted. My daddy always denied my requests. Therefore, I never felt that I had my father's full support, attention, and love. However, in recent years that changed. My daddy, who had for years been somewhat aloof in his parenting, became more hands-on and supportive – emotionally and financially. I was in my thirties when for the very first time, my daddy uttered the words, "I love you, Son!" I was startled beyond words – amazed. It was as if I had been waiting my whole life to hear those words from my daddy. Those words I received that day were the affirmation, authentication, and validation that every man needs from his father. From that day forward, whenever he said those four powerful words, I considered telling him what I believed that he actually already knew. Why did I feel the need to tell him? Because I wanted my daddy to fully know me, understand me, and continue to love me unconditionally as his son, as the man I truly am, and not the image that I had carefully crafted over the years. In my hotel room in Orlando, I dreamt that I told him. When I woke up that October Sunday morning, I knew the time had come. Rather than call and tell him right then, I decided that I would sit him, my mom, and my brother down while I was home for the Christmas holidays and have an honest and frank conversation with all of them...

Several weeks later – a week before Thanksgiving – I was at my home after an exhausting day when I received a phone call from my mother. She casually informed me that she was on her way to meet my daddy at the emergency room. I thought nothing of it. I had talked to him two days earlier; he said his side was hurting, so I thought that he was just going to the emergency room to have this pain checked out. I continued cleaning and also preparing for a date with my new beau. We were going to see the movie 2012. However, I decided to call my daddy for I just wanted to hear his voice and make sure he was fine. He did not answer his phone when I called; my cousin answered. "Where's my daddy?" I questioned.

"They are putting him in the ambulance!"

"Ambulance?!?!?!" I was confused; I didn't think that it was serious enough for him to need an ambulance to go to the hospital. I just assumed that my aunt or one of my cousins was taking him there. Still, I thought nothing of it...

While I awaited news of my daddy's health from my mother and cousin who promised to call me the moment they heard something, one of my best friends stopped by my house for a visit. We chatted while continued cleaning and preparing for my date with my new beau. I told my friend how excited I was about my new beau and seeing the movie 2012. In the middle of my conversation with my friend, I thought, I should call my daddy again. They should be at the hospital by now. I called my mama first; she didn't answer her phone. When I dialed my daddy's number, once again my cousin answered. This time, all I had heard was his crying. It still didn't register that anything was seriously wrong. He was so overwhelmed with emotion that he gave the phone to his wife. Immediately, I could tell that she too had been crying. I asked, "What's going on?" A nurse, she explained to me, had told them that from a preliminary examination, the doctors determined that my daddy had an aneurism and they had rushed him into surgery to drain the blood off his brain. "Where's my mama?" I inquired and learned that she was in the chapel with the rest of the family and was overwhelmed. I thought, The chapel? They take family members there when someone is about to.... Reality began to sink in, as I realized that my daddy's condition was more serious than I had thought. I asked my cousin's wife a question to which I really didn't want to know the answer: "Do I need come home?"

Through her tears, she answered. "Yes!"

I got off the phone with her and told my friend what had happened. My mind was racing a thousand miles a minute; I didn't know what to do. I didn't know how I was going to get home – it was a six-hour drive and I no longer had a car. My friend offered to drive me; I agreed reluctantly, for he had just started a new job and I didn't want him to get fired. I couldn't focus; my mind was all over the place so my friend packed a suitcase for me while I called my new beau to cancel our date and to explain to him exactly what was happening with my family. I told my beau that my best friend was going to drive me to my hometown.

He objected! "I wouldn't feel right being here with you there, going through this! I will take you!" Graciously, I agreed, and had my friend take me to his house.

Six hours later – a little after 2AM, we arrived at the hospital in my hometown. My entire extended family on my father's side was waiting along with my mama. I barely had time to greet anyone or introduce my new beau before they whisked me back to the Intensive Care Unit. I walked into the room along with my mama, a couple of cousins, and my beau and saw my daddy lying there on life support, with tubes seemingly running from everywhere. I fought back the tears and asked, "What are the doctors saying?" I was told that a blood vessel had ruptured in his neck, causing bleeding in the brain so the surgery was necessary to relieve the pressure. There was absolutely nothing we could do but wait and see how he progressed throughout the rest of the night and what the doctors would tell us in the morning. Now that I had arrived, the rest of my extended family went home. My mama, my beau, and I decided to spend the night at the hospital downstairs in the ICU waiting room. The three of us found reclining chairs right together. Exhausted, my mom and my beau went to sleep immediately, but I couldn't sleep! I was restless, and the loud snoring of two other individuals in this large room kept me awake as well. I decided to go back up to the upstairs ICU waiting room where my daddy was located. There was a computer in that waiting room; I needed to occupy my mind.

I was surfing the Internet when I felt someone enter the room. I turned around, but there was no one there. I continued surfing the web. Then all of a sudden, I heard my daddy call me by my nickname! "Bookie!" My ears perked up. Physically, I knew this was an impossibility; his motionless physical body was confined to a bed in the Intensive Care Unit, just around the corner from the waiting room. However, his spirit man was not confined to that bed. I refused to turn around and acknowledge the presence of his spirit, for doing so would force me to acknowledge that my daddy was vacillating between two worlds—the physical and the spiritual. His presence was confirmed, not by what I saw with my natural eyes, but by what I saw in the realm of the spirit. I was still facing the computer screen, but I saw my daddy--alive, vibrant, blissfully smiling and standing behind me. My natural man refused to accept what my spirit man was seeing. I defiantly told my father's spirit man, "NO!" That two-letter word said everything that I was thinking in that moment: You are not going to die! Go get in your body and get well, so you can go home! But the home I was thinking of was not the one to which he would be going. My daddy didn't reply; his spirit man simply left the room. I continued surfing the Internet for a while, but what little concentration I had was now broken.

Given my daddy's critical state, the doctors and nurses had graciously granted us free access, so we could see him anytime. I went to my daddy's room to see that his condition had not improved; the ventilator was doing ninety percent of the breathing for him. I could see the blood draining

123

from his head through the line the doctors inserted during surgery; we were told that if there was any hope of his condition improving, the blood flow would have to cease and he would have to physically respond to certain physical stimuli. He had been non-responsive since they brought him into the hospital. Tears began to stream down my face. I couldn't believe that in a matter of hours my world had turned upside down! I had gone from preparing for a date in one state to keeping vigil at my daddy's bedside in another state. I cried for the next two hours as the frightened little boy in me emerged. And I begged and pleaded with my daddy to wake up. I begged... I pleaded...I shook him! I begged... I pleaded...I shook him! I cried. I begged... I pleaded...I shook him! I cried. I begged... I pleaded...I shook him! I cried! I begged... I pleaded...I shook him! I begged... I pleaded...I shook him! I cried... Then I stopped crying! I stopped begging! I stopped pleading! I stopped shaking him! I realized that my daddy was not going to wake up. The doctor came in about 6AM that morning and confirmed what I was beginning to accept. My daddy would never wake up. I wasn't ready for my daddy to die, especially when we had become close again and I felt comfortable enough to reveal my truth to him. I would never have that chance...or so I thought...

The next morning, my beau and I were asleep in our hotel room when I got a phone call from my mother telling us to get to the hospital quickly! My daddy was leaving us. We jumped out of bed and rushed to the hospital. I arrived shortly before my mother, my aunt, and the rest of the family. My daddy's nurse informed us that his blood pressure was dropping rapidly. There was no doubt that he was leaving us. While family members continued to arrive to say their final goodbyes, I turned my attention to comforting my mother, controlling the crowd, and planning the funeral. My thought process was interrupted by my father's nurse who informed me that someone from hospital administration wanted to speak to me privately. She led me to the same ICU waiting room I was in the night I arrived, where three people were waiting. They first told me how sorry they were for my loss and then introduced themselves. They were from an organ and tissue bank affiliated with the hospital. They informed me that my daddy was in excellent physical condition and wanted to know if we would consider allowing my daddy to be an organ and tissue donor. Before they could even finish asking the question, without hesitation or reservation, I said, "Yes!" During my junior year in college, a high school friend was left brain dead after an auto accident. Her parents donated her organs and tissue, which helped save and enhance the lives of over a hundred individuals. This inspired me to become an organ and tissue donor. Lord knows that we can't take this body to heaven, so why not give the gift of life to someone whose journey on earth doesn't have to end so soon? Even though I said yes immediately, the decision was really not mine to make. It was my mother's. I brought her into the room and after thoroughly explaining the organ and tissue donation process to her, she agreed to allow my daddy's organs and tissue to be harvested, but she also wanted to get my little brother's input as well. We spoke with him, and the decision became unanimous.

Since my daddy was going to be a donor, he had to be kept alive so that the hospital harvest team could perform a series of tests that would indicate whether or not he had any brain activity. harvest team could not harvest his organs until the tests indicated that there was zero brain activity. However, the tests could not be performed until the next morning! "Great!" I exclaimed because I immediately thought of my little brother who was six hours away at college in another part of the state and had yet to see our daddy. He had to come home and he had to come now; time was of the essence! I told my cousin what needed to be done, and she sprang into action and got my little brother booked on the next flight home! The decision to allow my daddy to be an organ donor was a two-fold blessing. First and foremost, his organs and tissue could possibly enhance and save the lives of other people and secondly, it gave us the time to say our final goodbyes which is what my mama decided each of us needed to do.

I thought about my decision to reveal my truth to my father. I wonder if it even mattered at this point. For all practical purposes, he was brain dead. The essence of who he really was had already gone! Would he hear me or would I simply be talking to his body – a hollow shell - the house he used to live in – that was now being kept alive through life support. I talked it over with my beau, who encouraged me to have the conversation with my father anyway because I would never have the opportunity to have this conversation with him/his flesh again...

Monday...Tuesday...Wednesday...the brain flow tests continued to show that there was still some very small brain activity; however, it was not enough to hope for any recovery. As result, my daddy's organs and tissue could not be harvested even though other tests indicated that if he were taken off life support, he would expire quickly! My mother, brother, and I decided that we didn't want to wait another day; it was becoming too painful to look at my daddy in that bed hooked to that ventilator. We were informed that if we allowed him to expire naturally, the harvest team would whisk him to surgery immediately afterwards in hopes of savaging some of his organs and tissue. It would still be possible for his organs and tissue to save and enhance the lives of others. We all agreed, so along with the hospital staff, we set the time of 9PM for him to be removed from life support. We notified the family again! This is it! My daddy's final hours! Come say goodbye!

My mother had the nurses to move my daddy over to one side of the bed. She wanted to lay beside him and talk to him. This was the man she had loved and hated since she was sixteen years old. She had so much to say to him and not enough time to say it all! People came in and in out of the room while my mother lay beside her husband one last time. My brother said that he had said all he needed to say to Daddy when he arrived three days earlier; there was nothing more he wanted to say. So after my mother had her private time with Daddy, it was my turn...

I went into Daddy's room and closed the door. I got into bed with Daddy like I had done so many times when I was a little boy who was terrified of the dark. I sat there for a moment; I couldn't believe that I was in this moment – the final moments of my daddy's life. I didn't know where to begin or how to begin this all- important conversation, so I just began saying it:

Daddy, there is something I have been waiting to tell you for a while... I had planned to tell you this when I came home for Christmas, but since you won't be here, I have to tell you now... The reason I am telling you this now is because I feel that you should know, and that if no one else knows who you really are, your parents should know... To some degree, I already think you

*know, but I am here to tell you, Daddy, I am
a gay African-American man…*

This one-sided conversation with my daddy lasted almost a half-hour. I told him everything that I wanted to say but had not had the courage to say heretofore. I told him how as I child I needed and wanted him to take a more active part in my life. I thanked him for honoring the promise he made to me, which was to become more active in my brother's life. I thanked him for instilling in me a love for history and politics. I told him how I regretted that I waited so late to share my truth with him. The final two things I said to him were, "I hope I made you proud" and "I love you so much!" I left the room – not sure of how I felt, but yet glad I had the chance to have one last conversation with my daddy!

At 9PM, absent of any other family members, my mother, brother, and I watched as the respiratory therapist removed all the tubes and IV's, thus disconnecting my daddy from life support. My brother and I put our hands on Daddy's chest and felt his heartbeat as it became fainter and fainter and eventually stopped. Less than three minutes after the respiratory therapist disconnected life support, my daddy was gone...

Daddy died on the Wednesday before Thanksgiving. Needless to say, Thanksgiving was difficult. It was a personal test of one of my favorite scriptures – 1 Thessalonians 5:17 - "In everything give thanks for this is the will of God in Christ Jesus concerning you!" In the midst of coping with his death and planning the funeral, I praised God for even having a father to lose and all the wonderful things he had taught me. His funeral was the Saturday after Thanksgiving. Besides designing and writing the program and obituary, I had the honor, privilege, and pleasure of eulogizing my own father. The subject of my message was "Mission Accomplished" in which I likened my daddy to John the Baptist, whose sole mission in life was to affirm Jesus' message, authenticate his ministry, and validate him as the Son of God. I asserted that my daddy's mission on earth was accomplished because he did the same things John the Baptist did; he affirmed, authenticated, and validated his family, friends, and those in the immediate community.

For several weeks after my father's death, I had trouble sleeping. I slept with one eye open and one closed. The only time got any restful sleep during this time was when I was in bed asleep with my beau at his house. Why the trouble sleeping? I was waiting on my daddy to come see me, just as he had that night in the waiting room. Just as I had expected, my daddy came to see me! I spent one night at my beau's house and while in bed asleep, I had a dream: It was a fall night and my beau and I were on this riverboat cruise down the Mississippi River. We were standing and chatting on the top deck – the observation deck - enjoying the cool air when this man started walking toward us. He caught my attention; at first, I thought it was my cousin who looks like a younger version of my father, but as the man walked toward us, I realized that it was my father indeed! He looked young and vibrant as he was that night I saw him in the ICU waiting room. I was so shocked to see him; I was speechless. We stared at each other for a long while, neither of us saying a word. It was like I was frozen! It couldn't move! I just stared. Then suddenly, my father embraced me as he had never done before. As my daddy hugged me in my dream, I felt him hug me as I lay in the bed next to my beau. In reality – real time as we lay there, I saw the bedroom and my father standing over us as we lay in the bed. I can't explain it exactly, but somehow I was experiencing the same thing at the same moment as if I was consciously awake and he was actually there with us. My father leaned over the bed, picked me up and cradled me in his arms, touching various pressure points in my back. It was like he was holding me for dear life and did not want to want to let me go. However, after a long while, he did! The dream ended and so did the embrace and I remember, still asleep, being gently laid back in the bed beside my beau, and my father tucked his in little boy as he done so many times before...

I awoke the next morning with tears in my eyes and with a smile on my face. I still don't even know how to explain what I experienced. My daddy had come to see me in my dream, but also had also come to me in real and physical world. Even though he didn't say a word, the long embrace he gave me said it all! I knew my daddy had heard every word I said to him the night he died; he heard my confession that I am a same-gender loving African- American male. His embracing me while I lay in bed beside my beau was his way of saying, *"I affirm your message, I authenticate your ministry, I validate who you are: you are my son in whom I am well pleased, and I love you! You are still my child!"*

QUESTIONS OF RECONCILIATION

Tomorrow is not promised to any of us. I waited too long to reveal my truth to my father because I thought I had time. As you see in the story, time ran out for me, but it may not be too late for you. Consider these questions:

Is there a parent, friend, or family member you need to reveal your truth to because you desire for him/her to know the real you?

Are there reasons why you should not disclose your truth of your sexual orientation with your parent/friend/family member?

What effect do you think the knowledge of your sexuality would have upon them and your relationship with them?

What effect would be disclosing your sexuality have upon you? Is it best for them that you tell them the truth about your sexuality or is it best for them that you continue to conceal your truth?

Is it best for you to continue to conceal your truth? Why or why not?

If you should wait for the right season, then how should you plan for that time? If you decide to reveal your truth to them, will you do it all at once or in stages?

INSTRUCTIONS FOR DISCUSSION

After you have read the book and completed the Questions of Reconciliation, you may want to engage in an open dialogue with your same-gender loving counterparts – preferably those who have read the book and also responded to the Questions of Reconciliation. The group should have 5-7 participants and included other positive like-minded individuals who can be supportive of your journey. Please do not try to discuss the entire book in one sitting. Divide the book into at least 2 parts. The Questions of Reconciliation are designed to give voice to every group participant. Therefore, please allow each person to speak openly and freely. Please refrain from being judgmental, critical, or overstating your opinion. Be compassionate and listen! Again, the process of negotiating, reconciling, and integrating your spiritual and sexual identities is not a sprint – it is a marathon. Let the process of reconciling your spiritual and sexual identities continue...

Made in the USA
Columbia, SC
23 January 2023

10914276R00076